Going to the fair

Gill Tanner

Photographs by Maggie Murray
Illustrations by Sheila Jackson

Contents

A & C Black · London

Going to the fair

Have you ever been to a fair? People have been holding fairs for thousands of years. But before 1830, fairs were nothing like the ones you might visit today. Early fairs were meetings of people from different areas who gathered together in one place to trade. The earliest fairs we know about were held in Stone Age times. People gathered on hilltops to exchange tools, crops and animals.

▲ A modern fairground. Many of the rides and stalls have not changed a great deal in the last 100 years. In the foreground you can see the trucks and living vans of the people who own the rides and amusements.

At the turn of the century, going to the fair was something to look forward to, and to talk about for months afterwards.

During the Middle Ages, fairs became important events and could last several weeks. Fairs were held only in towns which had charters. A charter, which was a licence to hold a fair every year, had to be granted by the monarch or an important noble. In 1400, nearly 5,000 towns had such a charter. Charters were highly prized because a fair brought extra trade and wealth to a town.

By the turn of the century, fairs had changed completely and were much more like the ones we know today. Most of the merchants and traders had vanished. Instead, the main purpose of a fair was to provide entertainment. Fairs began to travel around the country, visiting towns and villages.

▲ Medieval fairs were often held on holy days, and opened with religious services and processions. Merchants came from all over the country and even from abroad to sell their goods. Around the edges of the fair jugglers, fire-eaters, clowns and actors entertained the crowds.

► The children studied this poster which was displayed in Nottingham before the Goose Fair in 1991. It explains some of the laws of the fair. Before a modern charter fair opens, a poster like this has to be displayed in the town or city.

Time-line

	pre-1880s	1880s	1890s	1900s	1910s	1920s
		Great great grandparents were born		Great grandparents were born		
Important events	**1876** Alexander Graham Bell invents telephone	**1888** Dunlop invents pneumatic tyre	**1890** Moving pictures start **1896** First modern Olympic Games	**1901** Queen Victoria dies. Edward VII becomes King **1903** Wright brothers fly first plane	**1910** George V becomes King **1914–18** World War I	**1926** General Strike in Britain
Fairground dates	**1805** Wombwell's Wild Beast Show starts travelling **1840s** George Twigdon invents the first 'Riding Machine' with wooden horses **1863** The first steam-powered roundabout made **1865** Frederick Savage of King's Lynn, Norfolk, makes steam-powered rides for fairs	**1882** A week-long new fair called the 'Hoppings', begins in Newcastle upon Tyne. The fair was started by the local Temperance Association whose members were opposed to the drinking of alcohol **1889** The Van Dwellers' Association is started by Mr F. Pedgrift, publisher of a theatrical newspaper called the *Era*. The Association later becomes the Showmen's Guild	Wombwell's Wild Beast Show is lit by electricity **1895** Wombwell's Wild Beast Show presents 'The Only Boxing Kangaroo in Europe' **1897** Showman Pat Collins takes out a patent for the method of electric lighting used on his roundabouts. His rides include a 'Channel Tunnel Railway'	Electric trams in many cities **1904** *World's Fair* newspaper first published by Frank Mellor **1909** Labour Exchanges introduced to give people information about job vacancies in their local area. These end the need for hiring fairs except in remote country areas	During World War I some fairs close. Many showpeople join the Forces **1917** The Showmen's Guild becomes a registered trade union	Candy-floss machines introduced from the USA **1924** Agricultural Wages Act passed. This stops the need for hiring fairs even in remote country areas **1929** Showman Pat Collins introduces the 'Wall of Death'. This has motor cyclists riding at high speed round the inside of a large wooden cylinder

This time-line shows some of the important events since your great great grandparents were children, and some of the events and inventions which have changed fairs and fairgrounds.

...randparents were born		Parents were born			You were born	
...930s	1940s	1950s	1960s	1970s	1980s	1990s

...36 Edward ...I abdicates. ...orge VI ...comes King. First ...evision ...oadcasts **...39** World ...r II starts	**1941** Penicillin successfully tested **1945** World War II ends **1947** First supersonic plane	**1952** Elizabeth II becomes Queen E II R	**1961** Yuri Gargarin first man in space **1969** Neil Armstrong first man on the moon	**1973** Britain enters the Common Market	**1981** First successful space shuttle flight	

...e first 'altzer' rides ...d 'Dodgems' ...pear. ...wer people ... to fairs ...cause of the ...verty and ...employment ...used by the ...reat ...pression'. ...ge increase ...the ...pularity of ...e cinema ...ds to a ...g-term ...cline in the ...pularity of ...rs	During World War II fairs are allowed to operate only in the daytime because of blackout rules. Many fairs stop working altogether **1941** The Showmen's Guild presents a Spitfire plane to the RAF ● Showmen stage the government's 'Stay-at-Home' holiday fairs **1946** Diesel engines introduced to drive rides and electric generators ● Diesel lorries used to pull wagons and transport rides	Children's rides include TV puppet star 'Muffin the Mule' ● New children's rides invented. These are miniature copies of adult rides, such as the 'Big Wheel' **1955** Disneyland opens in Anaheim, California, USA	Hot dogs and hot doughnuts introduced in fairgrounds as fast food	Alton Towers opens as a theme park	Travelling fairs invited to Bonfire Night displays. These put on huge firework displays and funfairs. They prove popular with a public now more aware of the dangers of fireworks ● Town square fairs for the first time are connected to town lighting supplies ● Corkscrew ride opens at Alton Towers	**1992** Live goldfish banned as prizes at Nottingham Goose Fair ● Euro Disney opens near Paris

5

Animals at the fair

Two hundred years ago, the main business at some of the most important fairs was buying and selling animals. Some fairs, such as Priddy Sheep Fair, Whibsey Horse Fair and Tavistock Goose Fair, were named after the creatures sold there.

By 1900, the popularity of the railways and the improvement in road surfaces made it easier for farmers to send their animals much longer distances to be sold. Local animal fairs became less important and were replaced by large agricultural shows. These were held on special show grounds and attracted hundreds of thousands of visitors.

Animals were also important fairground attractions. No medieval fair was complete without its dancing bear. In Victorian times, long before television and wildlife programmes, your great great grandparents were amazed by travelling menageries or collections of animals which they had never seen before, such as elephants, snakes and kangaroos.

▲ Geese were driven on foot to goose fairs such as the ones held every year in Nottingham and Tavistock. Farmers smeared the feet of the geese with tar and sand to stop them getting sore on the long walk.

A livestock fair at East Grinstead, Sussex, in 1900. There are still a few fairs where animals are sold, such as those held at Bridgwater and Priddy in Somerset. Other fairs which no longer sell animals, such as Nottingham Goose Fair, still keep their old names.

▲ James Wheatley owns 'Mouse Town' which he takes to various fairs. Children enjoy watching the uncaged mice moving among the little wooden houses and fairground. Today RSPCA inspectors visit all fairs to make sure that all animals are well treated.

One of the first fairground menageries, started by George Wombwell in 1805, contained only two boa-constrictors. Wombwell's shows eventually included performing lions and polar bears. By 1899, animal wonders such as miniature horses, giant bullocks and performing crocodiles were often seen at fairgrounds.

Gradually, as more people went to zoos, travelling menageries became less popular. Since 1945, animal quarantine laws, concern about the health of caged animals, and nature films on television have put an end to menageries and animal shows.

Hiring fairs

Today, if people need a job they may go to a Job Centre. There they can look at lists of jobs which are vacant in their area. Reading the job vacancy section in newspapers, or looking at Ceefax or Oracle on television, is also helpful because many employers advertise jobs there.

At the turn of the century there were no Job Centres. Many people, especially farm workers, could not read or write so advertising was not a suitable way to find workers. Instead, people who needed a job or a worker often went to a fair.

▲ Your local Job Centre advertises vacancies for jobs in your area.

▼ In 1888, workers came to this hiring fair to look for new jobs. Those on the left are talking to a farmer. In the middle the soldier, who is a recruiting sergeant, tries to persuade some young men to join the army.

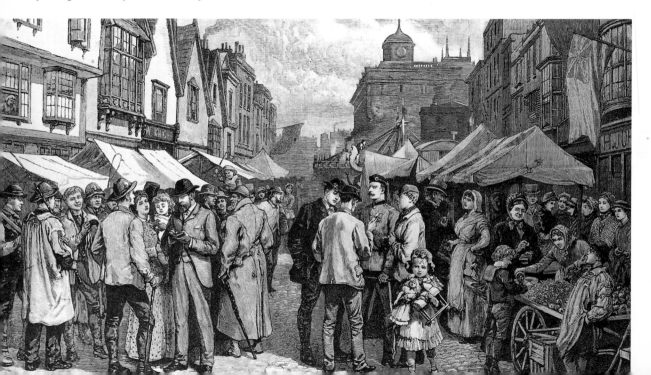

Hiring fairs, or 'mop fairs' as they were known, first started over 600 years ago, after one-third of the people in Britain died of a plague called the Black Death. King Edward III passed a law stating that workers had to present themselves at certain places each year to be hired at the same wages as those they were paid before the Black Death. The aim of the law was to stop the workers who had survived the plague from moving about in search of better paid jobs and, perhaps, spreading the disease.

Mop fairs were usually held at Michaelmas, in late September. Farmers and their families went to the fairs to find workers and to buy things for the farm. They spent any spare coppers on the exhibitions and entertainments. When a worker was hired, he or she was given a small sum of money, called a 'fastenpenny', by the new employer. The worker usually spent this money at the fair.

▲ This photograph was taken at the mop fair at Stratford-on-Avon in 1899. Each man is dressed in his best clothes and wears a 'mop' in the lapel of his jacket. 'Mop' is an old word for a twist of cord. By wearing this, a worker showed he was still for hire. Farmers looking for workers often examined their hands and felt their muscles to make sure they were strong and healthy.

'Pull on' and 'build up'

Between 1830 and 1900, new shops, trade exhibitions and agricultural shows made fairs less important as places for business. During this time, too, many people moved away from the countryside to find jobs in the new factory towns. The jobs were hard, and the factories depressing. The workers wanted to have some fun in their spare time.

The new travelling funfairs attracted huge crowds. These funfairs visited places where there had never been fairs before. New laws were passed to make sure that the fairs were safe. Council officers, called Clerks of Markets and Fairs, were made responsible for planning fairground sites.

▲ A photograph from about 1900 showing a traction engine hauling 40 tonnes of fairground equipment. Such long trains took hours to 'pull on' and unload.

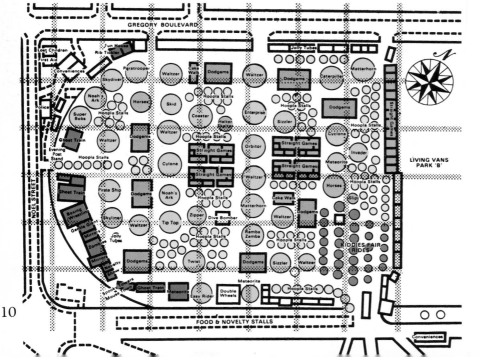

◄ The plan of the Nottingham Goose Fair in 1990. Plans like these are drawn up by the Clerk of Markets and Fairs, then checked by the Fire Brigade and Ambulance Service to make sure emergency vehicles will be able to get in if they are needed.

■ Show Road
○ Big rides
○ Traditional rides
▨ Dodgems
○ Hoopla stalls
▩ Straight games (rifles, coconut shies, arcades)
● children's fair rides

The arrival of a fair is called the 'pull on'. Before pull on starts, the ground is marked into numbered sites so the showpeople know where to assemble, or 'build up', their rides and stalls.

Pull on usually starts on the weekend before the fair is due to open. The bigger rides arrive first because they take many hours to build up. All the rides are checked by safety officers during and after build up. During the early part of the week the rest of the rides and stalls arrive, until, by mid-week, everything is in place and the fair is ready to open.

Most fairs visit the same places each year. Some fairground families have rented the same sites on the fairgrounds for generations. If you watch the arrival of a fair, you will see almost exactly what your great grandparents would have seen.

▲ Gradually the fairground takes shape. The rides are assembled and connected to trucks, called 'lighting sets', which carry electricty generators. After the rides have been tested, they are protected against overnight rain with canvas sheets.

◀ This girl tried filling in a stall application form. Each showperson has to send a form like this to the local authority of the area in which the fair is to be held. The local authority allocates sites on the fairground.

The Showpeople

The people who run the rides, stalls and games at a fair are called showpeople. Different generations of these show families have been working in fairs for hundreds of years. Many showpeople are related because their families have inter-married. The showpeople you see are likely to be the descendants of showpeople your great grandparents saw when they were children.

The routine of the travelling season for show families has hardly changed in the last hundred years. Each family visits at least forty fairs during the main travelling season between March and November. Trucks tow living vans and rides, games or stalls to the fair sites. The spaces for the vans and shows have to be booked in advance. One hundred years ago the vans and trailers were pulled by giant steam-powered traction engines.

◄ Many living vans are specially made for showpeople. Some have running water and flush toilets, and can be 20 metres long.

▼ Living vans as they were at the turn of the century. In those days the living vans were pulled by horses. The showpeople took all their children with them on their journeys.

12

At the turn of the century few children from show families went to school. By helping their parents, they learned how to run the rides, stalls and shows. But it was harder for them to learn to read and write while they travelled about. Sometimes teachers moved around with the fairs and ran travelling schools.

Today, some education authorities have special programmes to teach travelling children. Some younger children travel with their parents, but over half the older ones now go to boarding schools and only work in the fair during the holidays. In winter when the fair stops travelling, the children can go to local schools.

▲ 'Swag Alley', tucked away among the living vans, is a shopping place for the showpeople. They can buy prizes, sweets, coloured light bulbs, metal goods and dozens of other things they need from the stalls and trucks.

► Showpeople need easy-to-clean containers for water and for displaying and serving food. At the turn of the century, they bought copper or chrome metal goods from tinkers. Today the 'stainless-steel man' in 'Swag Alley' sells all the metal goods the showpeople need.

In the past, during the winter season when the fair did not travel, show families rented winter quarters on council or private land. They needed a lot of space for their traction engines, living vans, rides and repair workshops. But many of the sites once used for winter quarters have now disappeared, covered by new houses, shops and factories. Suitable winter quarters are becoming hard to find.

One organisation which helps showpeople is the Showmen's Guild of Great Britain. The Guild was originally formed in 1889 as the 'Van Dwellers' Association'. Its job is to protect its members, their businesses, their sites, their winter quarters and their way of life, and to tell the government about the special needs of travelling showpeople. The Guild also publicises local fairs and social events. It is a very important part of showpeople's lives.

▲ This photograph taken in 1904 shows the people who worked for one famous showman, A.C. Twigdon. They are sitting on a traction engine and trailer used for moving the rides. In 1897 another showman, Pat Collins, employed 450 people at his yard in Walsall to keep all his amusements in full working order.

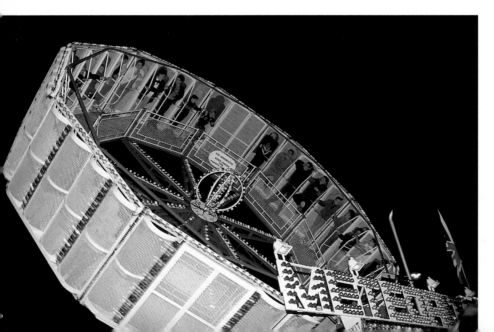

◄ Fast-spinning rides like this one could be dangerous. The Showmen's Guild is very concerned about safety at fairgrounds. The Guild arranges for approved safety inspectors to test all fairground rides each year. The owner of a ride has to supply a copy of the safety certificate when he or she applies for a site at a fair.

For hundreds of years showpeople found it difficult to contact friends in other fairs. In 1840 the 'Penny Post' started, but it did not help the showpeople because postmen could not deliver letters to moving living vans.

Instead, showpeople used messengers to carry their letters. One messenger was Frank Mellor. He visited many fairs selling lamps, bells, flares and metal goods which were made by his family at the Owl Lamp Works in Oldham. He was so often asked to take messages that, in 1904, he decided to start a newspaper just for showpeople. This newspaper, *World's Fair*, has been popular ever since.

◀ The Fairground Users' Safety Code was produced by the Showmen's Guild after discussions with the Royal Society for the Prevention of Accidents. It tells people how to enjoy themselves and be safe at a fairground.

▶ This girl ordered the *World's Fair* newspaper from the newsagent. She found that almost everything important to showpeople was included in it. She discovered messages, advertisements for goods, vacancies for sites at the big fairs, news and information from the Showmen's Guild. She learned that on the fairground the newspaper is called the 'Showman's Bible'.

Sideshows

Sideshows are an important part of any fair. They contain either mysteries, such as fortune tellers or mirror mazes, or exhibitions of unusual animals or people.

Among the sideshows seen ninety years ago were bearded ladies, strong men, boxers, waxworks, magicians, eight-footed cows, bioscopes (early cinemas), and the flea circus.

▼ Nottingham's 'Giant Girl'. In 1911 she weighed 185 kilos.

William Raynor, who has worked in fairs for many years, remembers:

'When we arrived at a fairground, I would go to the local newspaper and advertise for fleas. I would pay sixpence each for them. I had to stop in the end because I couldn't get enough fleas. Vacuum cleaners made houses too clean and sucked up all the fleas and their eggs.'

PROFESSOR ENGLAND'S
PERFORMING FLEAS!

Flea driving & drawing a hansom cab

à la Blondin

ADMISSION 2d EACH

◀ At the turn of the century people visited the flea circus because they could not believe that the tiny pests could be trained. In fact the fleas were just trying to escape from the fine wires which held them to tiny toys.

▲ These children had a look at the distorting mirrors from the turn of the century at Wookey Hole Caves and Mill. In 1900, most people had only small mirrors, so they found these huge, distorted reflections very entertaining.

At the turn of the century people or animals who were displayed in sideshows were called 'living wonders'. Many of those on show a hundred years ago were people who were deformed or handicapped in some way. In those days there were no disability pensions or equal opportunities. Displaying themselves at fairs was often the only way handicapped people could earn a living.

Today, people with disabilities share equal rights with the rest of society. But to the Victorians and Edwardians they were 'freaks' and fascinated the crowds who stared at them.

1890

▲ Captain Fisher was 'artistically tattooed' in 1885. It took twenty-four painful weeks to cover his body. Most sailors of the time had only small tattoos on their arms, so Captain Fisher was thought to be amazing when he was seen in sideshows during the 1890s.

Try your luck

Many of the games at fairs have hardly changed in the last hundred years. Simple throwing games with cheap prizes have been played at fairs since medieval times. Nearly all fairground games have a target of some kind which has to be hit or ringed.

Stalls for throwing games are still surrounded on three sides by canvas 'sheets' which stop the balls from being lost or hitting people outside the booth.

At the turn of the century, being skilful enough to win a prize in these games was a good way for a young man to impress his sweetheart or get a cheap present for her.

▲ This 'Aunt Sally' stall has painted human figures as targets. Notice the 'sheets' on the sides of the stall.

◀ This picture of a village fair was drawn in about 1900. Coconut shies have been popular on fairgrounds for many years. The coconut has always been a special prize. It was not something people would normally buy.

The prizes won on the stalls were called fairings. They were usually sweets, cheap toys or china ornaments. At the turn of the century the fairings most popular with children were 'ticklers', 'squirts' and bags of confetti.

Ticklers, fluffy sticks for tickling people, were sometimes made by the showpeople during the winter. Pieces of jute were dyed and fluffed, then nailed to sticks. A squirt was a water-filled tube of lead which, when squashed, shot out a jet of water. Squirts were not popular with grown-ups and were eventually banned from fairs because of complaints.

▲ Test-your-strength machines like this were popular in fairs at the turn of the century. Hitting the button with a mallet makes a metal striker slide up the groove towards a bell at the top. Many young men liked to use these machines to impress their friends.

▼ The modern fairings on this hoopla stall are just as difficult to win as the china and glass of 100 years ago.

Thrills and frights

The rides are the parts of the fair which have changed most in the last 150 years. The first roundabouts had to be light and small because they were worked by a team of boys running round them or by a boy turning a hand crank. The roundabouts also had to be small enough to be carried on carts drawn by horses.

▲ One of the earliest hand-cranked roundabouts, photographed in about 1850. The horses and chairs only went round, they did not go up and down as well. Roundabouts like this are called 'dobbies'.

By the turn of the century the introduction of steam-powered traction engines meant that roundabouts could be much larger and heavier. They were magnificent machines carrying luxurious gondolas and richly-carved horses. As they swirled round, their gold-leaf decorations, gilded barley-sugar columns, brightly-coloured paintings and glittering mirrors flashed and sparkled in the bright glow of electric lights.

▼ A steam-powered roundabout at Stratford-on-Avon Mop Fair in 1907. Roundabouts like this are called 'gallopers'. Notice the chimney in the centre for the hidden steam engine which turned the ride round.

Your great grandparents may have lived in a drab industrial town. Their first sight of electric lights may well have been at a fair. Fairs always look their most spectacular at night and, at the turn of the century, they attracted people from miles around.

As fairs became more popular, there was fierce competition between showpeople to find bigger and better rides. Manufacturers of fairground rides, such as Frederick Savage and George Orton, became famous for their fantastic roundabouts and zig-zag railways called switchbacks.

Modern rides are much lighter, faster and more thrilling than Victorian and Edwardian rides. But many fairs still have rides similar to those which your great grandparents enjoyed.

▲ At the turn of the century there were no adventure playgrounds. Many children had never been on a slide, so the helter skelter was a great thrill.

► Flashing mirrors and painted panels have always been used on fairground rides to hide the mechanical parts. The glittering centre post of this modern ride rises in the air with the cars spinning on the end of the arms. As it lifts, you can see the motor underneath.

'Showman's Style'

At the turn of the century many people in big cities lived in the smoke and pollution caused by heavy industry. The bright paintwork and glittering lights of the fairground made a welcome change from the gloom of their environment.

The horses and other animals on fairground rides were carved from wood. Many of the most skilful wood carvers also made figureheads for sailing ships. The most famous wood carvers of all were Arthur Anderson and C.J. Spooner.

▲ An unfinished wooden carving from Arthur Anderson's workshop in Bristol.

▼ The gallopers on this ride were carved in Arthur Anderson's workshop over one hundred years ago.

The animals were painted freehand in a bold, colourful way called 'Showman's Style', but each wood carver and painter had his or her own version of the style. When the painting was finished, gold leaf was added to make the rides shine in the sunlight and glow in the lamplight.

Today the panels for the sides of the rides are moulded from fibreglass and painted with metallic paints. These paints are cheaper and easier to use than gold leaf.

Modern fairground painters often paint futuristic themes but still use the old Showman's Style. Next time you visit a fair, see if you can tell the old rides from the new ones.

▲ This galloper, which is on display at Wookey Hole Caves and Mill, is actually a carving of C.J. Spooner done in 'Showman's Style'.

▲ A modern piece of fairground artwork moulded in fibreglass and decorated with metallic paint in 'Showman's Style'.

► Carvings by Spooner on the centre panels of a ride of gallopers. Panels like these hid the machinery of the roundabout. The edges, where the two panels meet, are cleverly carved to form a complete coat of arms which hides the gap.

23

Fast food

Do you know the old nursery rhyme 'Simple Simon met a pie-man, going to the fair . . '? The pie-man's mutton pies were the fast foods of the medieval fairgrounds.

At the turn of the century, fairground food stalls sold hot chestnuts and jacket potatoes cooked on braziers. Mrs Norton remembers a fair on Wanstead Flats in East London eighty years ago:

'Hot roast chestnuts in a bag warmed your hands. You cracked them and ate them as hot as you could. A bag cost a penny.'

At some fairs a whole ox was roasted each day. In the evening the ox was carved up and people bought portions to eat. Your great grandparents also enjoyed eating toffee apples, and gingerbread shapes with gold sugar decorations.

◄ Roasting an ox at the Mop Fair, Stratford-on-Avon, in 1899. The spit had a wagon wheel on the right-hand end so the heavy piece of meat could be turned from time to time. Notice the steam traction engine in the background.

► This modern food stall sells a selection of fast foods. The stainless steel containers and display units are easy to sterilise and keep free from germs. While a fair is being built up, an official from the local health department inspects the stalls.

24

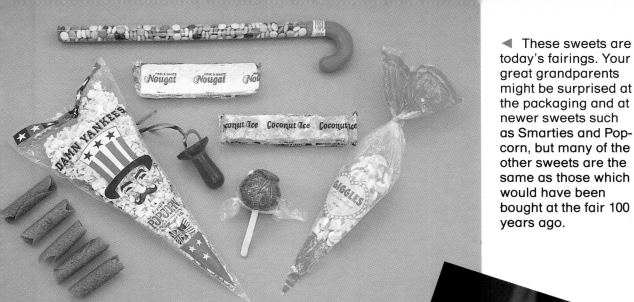

◀ These sweets are today's fairings. Your great grandparents might be surprised at the packaging and at newer sweets such as Smarties and Popcorn, but many of the other sweets are the same as those which would have been bought at the fair 100 years ago.

▶ Candy floss is made from melted sugar. It was eaten many years ago in India, where it was sold in lengths draped over sheets of paper and known as 'budikabahl' or 'old man's hair'. Nowadays, candyfloss is made with the help of an electrically powered spinning drum, first brought from America in the 1920s, which spins the sugar strands on to a stick.

Most traditional fairground foods are sweet because sugar keeps well and does not go mouldy. The sweets sold at fairs are usually colourful or are displayed in bright packaging. This vivid colouring is called the 'Flash' by showpeople, and it is one of the things that make fairs brighter and more magical than daily life.

Some fairs were famous for special foods, such as Grantham Fair for its gingerbread. Nottingham Goose Fair is famous for its cockerels on sticks. These are made of aniseed rock in the shape of the cockerels on the roundabouts.

▶ Traditional cockerels on sticks like this one have been sold at Nottingham Goose Fair for over 150 years.

25

Music

Music is important at the fairground because it attracts people to the fair and lets everyone know that the rides and shows are open for business. Music also covers the noises made by the machinery driving the rides.

At the turn of the century, large exhibitions or shows, such as Wombwell's Wild Beast Show, had their own brass bands. Elsewhere on the fair your great grandparents might have tapped their feet to the sounds of Scottish pipers, barrel organs, a type of hand organ called a hurdy gurdy, a small orchestra or a single fiddler.

In about 1870, showman Pat Collins introduced the first fairground organ from Europe at the cost of £1000. It was advertised as a:

▲ This organ is the centrepiece of a ride of gallopers made in 1884 by Frederick Savage, a famous manufacturer of roundabouts. The sound of the organ still makes people stop and stare, and may even encourage them to take a ride.

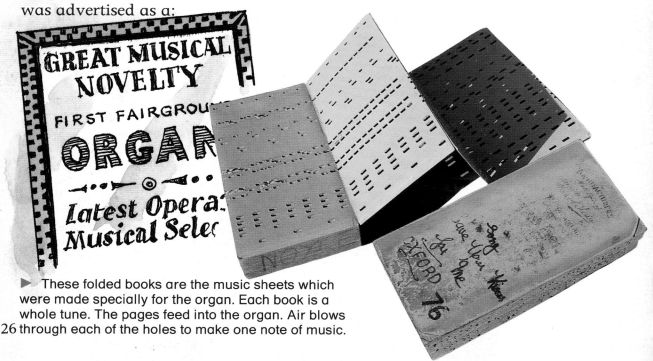

▶ These folded books are the music sheets which were made specially for the organ. Each book is a whole tune. The pages feed into the organ. Air blows through each of the holes to make one note of music.

26

It was such a great success that many other showpeople bought organs for their rides. The organs were beautiful machines and they did not have to be paid wages. They were driven by steam and their huge fronts were decorated with carved figures, bright paintings and hundreds of lights.

Modern showpeople also use loud music and noisy special effects. Many rides have electronic controls which make the lights flash in time to the popular tunes of the day. You will never hear sad music at the fair.

▼ A musical show at the Stratford-on-Avon Mop Fair in 1908. The girls sit on swings decorated with paper flowers while they sing popular songs of the time.

'Pull down' and 'pull off'

Eventually the fair had to come to an end. As soon as the last note of music sounded, the showpeople started to take down the rides and booths. They called this 'pull down'.

The equipment was taken down and loaded on to trailers. Traction engines then pulled the trailers to the fair's next destination.

Your great grandparents were probably very disappointed when they went out on Sunday morning to find the fair had disappeared overnight, leaving hardly a trace.

Mr G.C.A. Austin, Clerk of the Nottingham Fair, wrote in his memoirs in 1896:

'When ladies in Sunday apparel, accompanied by silk-hatted gentlemen set out for morning service, all traces of the fair had vanished. The market place was empty; the side streets nearby were cleared of the scores of living vans which had been standing there. But on the site of the menagerie, there lingered the unmistakeable odour of animals.'

▼ The large rides are the first to leave. Like all fairground rides, they are designed to fold up so they can be towed to the next site.

▲ The gallopers which your great grandparents may have ridden were designed to be taken to pieces in sections. Each section is numbered and has its own place in the trailer.

◀ The most popular fairs today are the funfairs and theme parks which are based on permanent sites. Because they don't have to tour around, these fairs have spectacular rides such as this 'Corkscrew' at Alton Towers, which offer thrills and frights never dreamed of 100 years ago.

Today some rides and booths can be packed up very quickly and sent to the next fairground. Setting out on the journey to the next fair is called 'pull off'. Modern machinery is much faster at transporting equipment than the traction engines of the turn of the century. These days the rides arrive at the new site the following morning.

Other rides and booths are packed up ready for transporting early the next morning. Work often goes on all through the night. If there is no hurry, some rides may be left standing until the following day.

All the rides and booths are designed to fold up so they can travel on the roads. Some rides are built on trailers. Parts of the platform fold up until the trailer becomes narrow enough to be pulled behind a van or truck.

▲ After a modern fair closes, the main problem is clearing all the litter left by the thousands of visitors.

How to find out more

Start here	To find out about...	Who will have...
Old people	Fairs at the turn of the century	Old photos, scrap books, memories, souvenirs
Museums	Old things to look at and possibly handle	Displays about local fairs, machinery and people at fairs. Fairings
Libraries	● Loan collections ● Reference collections ● Information to help your research ● Local history section	● Books to borrow ● Useful addresses, guidebooks ● Newspapers and guides to look at; photographs of local fairs; tape recordings of old people remembering their visits to fairs
Junk shops	Fairings, and fairs near your home	Old magazines showing fairs. Postcards, old photos, fairings
Local records office	Fairs held in your area 100 years ago	Council reports of fairs dating back 100 years. Copies of fair charters or statutes if the town has one
Markets and Fairs Department of your local council	The rules for fairs in your town	Leaflets and information about fairs in your area. Photographs and fair plans
World's Fair newspaper	Fairs today, dates, new rides, new inventions	Information about fairs today and new EEC rules
Showmen's Guild	Traditional fairs around the country	Leaflets on fairs and safety code. Information on how rides work and on the lives of showpeople
Local newspaper archives	Your local fair and its history. Your local fair today	Photos and stories about fairs. The opening ceremony. Advertisements

Who can tell you more?

They can. Use a tape recorder for recording their memories. Handle anything they show you with great care and, if they lend you something, label it with their name and keep it somewhere safe

The curator or the museum's education officer. Many museums have bookshops and a notice board where you can look for further information

- The librarian
- The reference librarian
- Ask the archivist for the name and address of the local history society

The owner. Specialist shopkeepers are very enthusiastic and knowledgeable about their stock. They may know of people connected with local fairs

The archivist. Phone to make an appointment. Documents may be photocopied by arrangement only

The market officer. Do not contact him or her just before or during a fair. Your teacher may be able to arrange an interview to talk about the job

Your newsagent can order it for you

The secretary of the local Guild section. Your teacher may be able to arrange for a showperson to visit your school

The information desk

Places to visit

The following places have displays, reconstructions or exhibitions connected with fairs:

Avoncroft Museum of Buildings, Stoke Heath, Bromsgrove, Hereford and Worcester B60 4JH. Tel: 0527 31886 (phone first to check if Tom Clarke's Waggon is on view yet)
The Black Country Museum, Tipton Road, Dudley, West Midlands DY1 4SQ. Tel: 021 557 9643
Brewhouse Yard Museum, Castle Boulevard, Nottingham NG1 1FB. Tel: 0602 483504
Burton Court, Eardisland, nr Leominster, Hereford and Worcester. Tel: 05447 231
Hollycombe Steam Collection, Hollycombe Steam and Woodland Garden Society, Iron Hill, Liphook, Hampshire GU30 7UP. Tel: 0428 724900
The Lynn Museum, Market Street, King's Lynn, Norfolk PE30 1NL. Tel: 0553 775001
Museum of East Anglian Life, Abbot's Hall, Stowmarket, Suffolk IP14 1DL. Tel: 0449 612229
Museum of Oxford, St Aldate's, Oxford OX1 1DL. Tel: 0865 815559
Tewkesbury Museum, 64 Barton Street, Tewkesbury, Gloucestershire GL20 5PX
The Thursford Museum, Thursford, Fakenham, Norfolk NR21 0AS. Tel: 032877 477
Tom Varley's Museum of Steam, Todber Caravan Park, Gisburn, nr Clitheroe, Lancashire. Tel: 02005 332
Wookey Hole Caves and Mill, Wookey Hole, Wells, Somerset BA5 1BB. Tel: 0749 72243

Useful addresses

Fairground Association of Great Britain, 38 Stratford Avenue, May Bank, Newcastle under Lyme ST5 0JS
Fairground Heritage Trust, 34 Sackville Gardens, Hove, Sussex BN3 4GH (charity to preserve fairground heritage)
Fairground Society, The Rutland Cottage Music Museum, Millgate, Whaplode St Catherines, Nr Spalding, Lincolnshire
RSPCA Head of Education, Manor House, The Causeway, Horsham, West Sussex RH12 1HG (for information about the RSPCA interest in working animals)
Showmen's Guild of Great Britain, Central Office, Guild House, 41 Clarence Street, Staines, Middlesex TW18 4SY (for address of the local section and local information on fairs in your area)
Society of Independent Roundabout Proprietors, The Bungalow, Sibthorpe Hill, Nr Tuxford, Nottinghamshire (owners of historical roundabouts)

Index

Published by A & C Black (Publishers) Limited
35 Bedford Row
London WC1R 4JH
© 1992 A & C Black (Publishers) Ltd

ISBN 0–7136–3635–1

A CIP catalogue record for this book is available from the British Library.

Filmset by August Filmsetting, Haydock, St Helens
Printed in Italy by L.E.G.O.

Acknowledgements

The author and publisher would like to thank: the late Dolly Whiting for the idea; the Showpeople and Swag Alley traders at Nottingham Goose Fair 1991; Bernard Mitchell, past secretary Section 8, The Showmen's Guild; Monica Stoppleman; Nottingham Museum Staff, Phylis Norton; Colin Lloyd of Kando; Mike Burchall, Clerk for Markets and Fairs, Nottingham; Supt. Brown RSPCA; Pamela Wood of the Castle Museum, Nottingham; Paquita Webb and the staff and owners of Wookey Hole Caves and Mill; Ruth Prior, Amy Hemmings, John Dourneen, Helen Steele and Maureen Steele.

Photographs by Maggie Murray except for p29 (top), Alton Towers; p9, 24 (top), Benjamin Stone Collection, Birmingham Library; p25 (middle) John Heinrich; front cover (inset), p8 (bottom), 18 (top), 20 (bottom), 27 (bottom), The Hulton Picture Company; p7 (top), 21 (top), The University of Reading, Institute of Agricultural History and Museum of English Rural Life; p13 (bottom), 23 (left) Light Work; p2 (bottom), 10 (top), 14/15, 16 (top), 20 (top), Nottingham Local Studies Library; p12 (bottom), 18 (bottom), Mary Evans Picture Library; p10 (bottom), Nottingham City Council; p8 (top), Brenda Prince/Format